THE FARMER ENTREPRENEUR

SEED

How farmers can rule the world

Santhosh Lakshmanan

INDIA · SINGAPORE · MALAYSIA

to the Farmer

CONTENTS

PART-I: THE PIECES. THE INPUT.

PART-II: THE WHOLE, THE OUTPUT

PART-III: THE MOVEMENT

PREFACE

I had always known about the day-to-day and economic problems of farmers. But it was in the years 2000 and 2001 that I could get a peek into the severity. Still in college, I would visit the library daily to read The Hindu. Reading the op-ed pages, particularly those pieces written by rural affairs journalist P. Sainath, I could feel the numbness of the heart. This book is the product of that numbness. Ever since, my whole existence has been acutely attuned to the suffering and helplessness of the farmer.

It has been almost a decade since I started on this journey in late 2014. There have been many experiences and learnings; most important of all for me was that I could see the societal opportunity right in front of me - an opportunity that at first seemed to be good enough to only make the life of a farmer bearable, comfortable and enjoyable; but gradually expanded, like the inflation of a balloon, to areas well beyond the realms of agriculture into trade, business and justice.

In line with Mahatma Gandhi's maxim 'Be the change you want to see in this world', I set forth on understanding how to be a farmer and an entrepreneur. Much water has flown under the bridge since. Suffice to say, my efforts were phenomenally successful and fulfilling at the personal level but were insufficient at the societal (my home district) level. The initiatives, carefully built MVPs (Minimum Viable Products), proved successful in realising their objectives; the theories were completely tested and proved valid. But the transition to societal change did not materialise – the limited bootstrapped resources could only go that far. The next step is to take this vision of *'The Farmer Entrepreneur'* to the world to suck in the energies of the cosmos to realise its fullest potential.

But there are too many things that could be written; writing them all in one long book could be counter-productive. There are also many doubts - will this book and its contents be seen as useful or practicable, will it drive the intended change, will it resonate with the farmer and the larger society? Ultimately, I could not let myself not put it out to the world, for the opportunity was critically significant to society. So, I broke down the tome: book-1 (Seed) is kind of the introduction to the whole edifice and thought of that of 'the farmer entrepreneur'. It is the seed that I hope will take root and grow. Books-2 and -3 may follow.

Book-1 intends to set up a new frame of reference as to what can be with respect to the life of a farmer. It does not seek to take the current situation and replace weaker pieces with stronger ones. Again, it sets up a new frame of reference. But setting this new reference is not as hard as it sounds and is in fact much easier to understand and implement to remedy the current situation.

If book-1 is well received, I will have the motivation to write book-2, which will be the full-fledged how-to of how this vision can be executed at the ground level; I'm sure some amount of movement would have happened if and when Book-2 comes to life. Book-3 will be a portrayal of the future – a future where the fulcrum of creating economic wealth, protecting natural wealth and securing cultural wealth will rest durably and assuredly with the farmer.

Undoubtedly, this book is for the farmer - the one who had been, the one who is and the one who will be. It is also for someone who is interested in agriculture and rural eco-systems. It is also for those who are interested in sustainability of the environment and our social systems. It is for policymakers and well-wishers of farmers.

Santhosh Lakshmanan

4-September-2024

www.TheFarmerEntrepreneur.org

ACKNOWLEDGEMENTS

There have been many people who have advised, helped and prodded me on in this long, tiring and emotional roller-coaster. Specifically, I would like to mention Jayakumar from Sholur village who has been a pioneer in natural farming for his support and kindness, the Pororai brothers – Suresh and Prabhu Nanjan - for their entrepreneurial efforts and forthright suggestions which helped me tide over many lows, Magamaga Belliappan from Kil Kundah village for his help in all logistics matters in the early stages of this endeavour, my brothers in my village for their zest in handling all sales and billing activities for many months, an erudite Vignesh Shankar for being my sounding-board on many topics, Sudipta Das for his resolute support and advice, my erstwhile employees for their dedication to their work, and my wonderful family for being with me despite the tough circumstances. I would have quit this endeavour long before had it not been for the unfailing support of my brother Jagdish.

PART-I:

THE PIECES. THE INPUT.

Chapter - 01

THE CURRENT STATE

One's interest may be piqued by reading the sentence under the title - how farmers can rule the world. The social prognosis of the farmer is not a promising one. The general belief is that farmers are poor, have to work very hard to make ends meet and do not have a chance to participate in the wonderfully modern world governments and policymakers are about to deliver. So, the common man (not the farmer) blinds himself to everything that has to do with the farmer except, of course, food.

That anyway has to come from the work of the farmer and for that the common man is genuinely interested in the welfare of the farmer and sometimes even takes her side (as say, in some protests). The impression he has of the farmer's life is certainly not favourable. So, he works hard to secure a job that is far from farming, and more importantly "educates" his children so that they have a "good" job. In today's milieu the farmer embraces this ideal more than the common man. For the farmer, there is no future in farming. She continues to farm only because her circumstances do not allow her to venture out of farming and if given a chance to get out of farming with a small regular income, she might take it with both her hands.

This state is, admittedly, extremely distant from ruling the world.

Chapter - 02

THE IDEAL

உழுதுண்டு வாழ்வாரே வாழ்வார் மற்றெல்லாம்
தொழுதுண்டு பின்செல் பவர்

This is a couplet from Thirukural, written two millennia ago by Tamil saint-poet Thiruvalluvar. It says that the one who tills the land and grows his own food is the one who truly lives life with freedom and all the others live lives wretched and always dependent. The current situation is at complete odds with that sense of freedom and power. It appears governments take all the steps that could solve these problems and it appears civil society is well behind the welfare of farmers but the problems seem to grow unabashedly what with news of farmer suicides and farmer indebtedness hogging the limelight for long periods of time only to be condemned to the back pages for want of novelty.

After researching these issues and employing various models/ solutions within a limited geographic area for more than nine years on agricultural production, entrepreneurship and related areas, this author believes that solutions to farm distress are well within the control of farmers. Not only can farmers relieve their financial problems, they can do a lot more. The farmer can control every lever of the economy and so can dispense justice and opportunity to all sections of people, particularly the weaker ones.

How? There are some ground rules or principles to take us (the farmers) in that direction, some key focus areas to always be mindful of, and a broad method that will get us there.

Chapter - 03

THE PRINCIPLES

There are four core principles.

Principle 1: Only farmers and no one else can change the fortunes of farmers.

This by far is the most important principle. As they go about their routine work many, if not most, farmers, today implicitly expect a lending hand from other stakeholders in multiple ways. An equal relationship between the farmer and the other stakeholders, say for instance marketing intermediary, has transformed into dependence by the farmer on the intermediary so much so that the market intermediary has come to believe that he is doing a favour to the farmer by auctioning farm produce. Likewise, all others that the farmer deals with treat a small farmer as the undeserving beneficiary of their business. But make no mistake - the farmer is the fuel to the economic engine and is the only essential entity in these transactions. But of everyone, the farmer is loath to believing that - she feels she is too small for anything of significant change. Farmers depend on everyone but themselves. As long as this belief persists in farmers, it will be hard to change the current state. Farmers need to understand that the other party is here to serve her and she has to wrest the power. Farmers are a proud species. It is with a heavy heart they stand at the receiving end of transactions. Only they have the power to change their fate.

Principle 2: Farmers are the best decision makers; given a set of constraints they take the best decisions every day.

Taking firm decisions is the hallmark of great entrepreneurs and that the farmer has been doing for ages. Be it considering the right time for sowing/ harvesting based on various factors like prices or be it selling of the land and cattle to meet expenses for the child's education or wedding, the farmer by virtue of their occupation has got into the habit of taking tough decisions every day. The feedback loop is short and the decisions get better. Then how are they at such a poor plight? The world keeps changing ever so slowly and one day when the farmer wakes up it has changed so dramatically that it is impossible to get a handle on it to serve their purpose. Recall the story of the frog in the kettle that has been kept on fire. The water rises in temperature and until it is boiling the frog does not realise it.

The business landscape continues to change at a rapid pace. Many of the companies in the top 500 list 30 to 50 years ago are not in that list today. When that is the fate of professionally run million-dollar organizations, what can be said about the fate of the small farmer? Combine this with the power and influence of big capital today. Input costs have risen prohibitively, labour is expensive and tough to manage and farm gate prices are ever so in a downward spiral adjusting for inflation and expenses. It is only thanks to the resourcefulness of the small farmer that she continues to be in business. All other experts (in their own fields, not in agriculture) – economists, business magnates, industry stalwarts, professionals etc. - would have run away from such a state of business. But is it only about business for the farmer? What about her land, her culture, her people, her forests, her cattle, her ponds and natural environment. It is only for these that she is standing in what appears a losing battle. That question of whether to quit is a decision she takes often, once in a while hoping that things will become clearer or that farming will become a bit more lucrative. From small to the big far-reaching decisions, the farmer is head and shoulders above everyone else when it comes to taking the best decisions. She only needs a handle to make sense of the new world and when they have it, their powerful decision-making skills will elevate them to the top-most level.

Principle 3: Farmers can control the foundations of entire economies and it only takes a spark to set them on this path.

Say there is a village of 100 families of which 70 are chiefly into farming. The others are professionals, traders, labourers, shopkeepers, service providers, teachers etc. If the farmers are earning well, these non-farmers make good profit out of their business. Even when the farmers make losses, these professionals continue to profit though the profits are slightly lower. All sections of non-farmers are entirely dependent on the farming community for earning profits; so, the whole economy in the village (just as in the whole country) is dependent on the farmer but the farmer is losing money due to high prices of inputs supplied by the trader and poor returns. The farmer begins to ask for debt and the only people he can ask are the trader and the lender because they are the ones making profits. Sometimes the farmer is not able to repay the debt; so, the lender and the trader take ownership of the farm. The sources of income for the non-farmer have increased now – farm rent, interest on debt, and his main occupation - while for the farmer the only source that continues to shrink is farming. For a farmer to enter into these businesses, entry barriers are stupefyingly high including capital needs, acquisition of new customers, understanding the new business, nuances of the business, etc.

But when farmers in that village combine to start a business, all of them will be willing customers for the new business for it is their own business. Of course, the business has to be run as though it was being run by the non-farmer trader. There are other bottlenecks too which can be overcome but the biggest benefit is acquiring customers en-masse from day one of starting the business. Which other large section of people has this advantage? There can be many other hurdles too, but the business can get going from day one.

Principle 4: Self-reliance, in anything and everything, is the way forward.

In Economics, the four factors of production are land, labour, capital and organisation. The widely accepted wisdom and truth is that the ones who control these factors will enjoy the maximum wealth in the world. Also, no individual has created massive wealth by standing alone. If he has one of the factors, then he has joined with the others who have the other factors to generate wealth; the wealth thus generated is then distributed among those who brought in the factors.

In modern times, farmers have had control over their land. Traditionally, labour has come from the farmer's own family, and he has used his own capital always. Therefore, land, labour and capital have always been with the farmer. The only reason for his poor status is the absence of the fourth factor – organisation or Entrepreneurship on a broader scale i.e. organisation along with others.

While taking control of organisation, the underlying motif must be a complete reliance on the self. The self here is the body of farmers – not the individual, not the village, but beyond that. The farmer needs to come together across regions to capitalise on this opportunity. The guiding principle must be complete self-reliance. It may sound far-fetched now but if farmers need telecom services, they will own a telecom company. If they want to give wings to their athletic or sporting abilities, they will run full-fledged sporting leagues to identify and groom talent inherent in their children and exhibit it on the international stage. They will not depend on the other to give them a hand; they will join hands to create what they want. If the challenge is small, they will overcome it with the village company; for tougher challenges, depending on what it takes to overcome the challenge, they will unite at the district- or state- or regional-level.

Chapter - 04

PILLARS OF ACTION

What are the most important requirements that will help us in moving and succeeding in this direction? What do we need to have before venturing in this direction? Broadly, these are awareness, unity and technology – the three pillars of action and the focus areas.

By far the single most important reason for the poor economic status of the farmer and that has a devastating cascading effect on the farmer's life is the lack of **awareness**. Ever since the European explorers invented the concept of a company, the spread and influence of capital and knowledge has reached the farthest corners of the world. In the past 40 years or so, advances in information technology have been so rapid that if a person who went into coma then came out of it today, he will hardly be able to make sense of the world.

The world has evolved beyond recognition and continues to evolve at an exponential pace; but here we have the small farmer in his own little world like a little lamb that believes in the kindness of the marauding wolf. Ignorance may be bliss but not of the imminent arrival of the wolves, unfettered capitalist forces. Farmers are losing their land, moving out of their villages, forgetting their culture, living in cities, working as coolies and unskilled hands and losing their peace of mind.

What are the absolute basics that the farmer must be aware of? The legal considerations and options around their core occupation of agriculture; the broader provisions of the companies act and the possibilities it entails; the power of information technology and its basic features and a basic understanding of the broader business landscape.

Farmers must be aware that to fix their problems they must come together and that they can come together to form a company/

farmer's company/ co-operative that is firmly in their control. They must know that it is a very simple administrative task to start a company; starting a company is neither a tough task nor an expensive one.

Farmers must be aware that in order to keep costs low and run operations efficiently they need to come together at different levels – village, district, etc.

Farmers must know that anyone can own and run profitable businesses. The biggest business houses are able to succeed because they employ the best minds. When farmers can come together, they can do the same – they only need to clarify their objectives and let the employees deliver results; they can employ specialists and professionals to get things done and fulfil their goals and objectives.

Farmers need to realise that they are the only large section of people that have not been able to utilise the power of information technology (IT), which is the greatest enabler of success today, to empower themselves. Most other sections like traders, corporates, educationists, professionals, etc. have embraced technology and empowered themselves by leaps and bounds. Most of these sections cannot run their businesses today without IT but farmers are still very far from IT.

Unity

While improving awareness is only one part of the battle won, another is one piece that is the toughest to bring about – **unity** in business. Farmers cannot build a conglomerate that is owned and profits a few. But they can build a conglomerate that benefits the farmers who participate in building the conglomerate. This leads us to the PPP model – Participate, Perform, Progress.

Unity will need to bloom at different levels, the lowest being that at the village level. Agriculture is vastly different across the various regions. It is intricately intertwined with the culture of people, the weather patterns, history, geography, soil conditions, surrounding natural environment, etc. Even within one district the nature of farming can vary vastly. Within a village, variance is limited and because of the broad set of similarities among the inhabitants of that village, it is easiest to have common agenda and goals to share the benefits.

Farmers may be united in protesting and submitting requests to governments. But that unity has been futile and an exercise that results in more desperation. The only unity that is needed is that which will help them organise themselves into business powerhouses. That unity will need to begin at the village level and spiral outwards.

Technology

When this level of awareness and unity grows, the benefits start to emerge and those villages that are particularly more progressive roll-up to drive the efforts that brought them success at their village to the higher and geographically broader levels. This can be structured in a robust and flexible way. The third pillar - technology - in the hands of the aware and united farmer is the easiest to build but the greatest enabler of change and opportunity. Its presence will be unnoticeable initially but as the movement gains momentum it will pervade the entire continuum of the farmer's actions.

To be more specific, in the early stages, we will need information technology more than any other technology. Internet, e-commerce, social media and many other disruptive phenomena that have sprung up in the past two to three decades have all been built on and leverage information technology. The movement of information across boundaries happens almost instantaneously today. While all sections of society have benefited from IT, farmers as a community need to know that technology is just a tool that anyone can use to benefit themselves. In this case, technology can empower the farmer community tremendously at very low relative costs. They must trial and test it once to truly understand the power of technology.

Chapter - 05

THE METHOD

At every level of operation in this movement there is one generic method that helps to simplify the maze and aids in the better understanding among all stakeholders – participate, perform and progress. Any entity must first participate in the next higher-level entity. For example, a farmer participates in the activities/ operations of the village group. Then, the farmer performs according to the expectations set by the village group. For example, the village may expect that a farmer must grow and make available 10 tonnes of a produce across three months for sales. In the progress stage, those entities that consistently meet or exceed expectations are rewarded higher than the other. Notice here that these expectations are set at the village level and so every farmer is by default a part of the deliberation process. Unless most farmers agree to the standards/ expectations, the expectations cannot pass through.

The generic method essentially rewards those farmers and groups that participate and perform well in building the conglomerate. For a conglomerate, think of a few big business groups – there are hundreds of companies under their holding companies. There is a need to identify the most progressive farmers and groups who have brought themselves success and who can then help bring success to other farmers and groups. At the same time there is a set of benefits that progressives deserve for their work; benefits can range from monetary to experiential to new opportunities. The matching of the progressive entity to the benefit will happen at different levels from the village up and there must be clarity to this matching for all stakeholders to understand. For instance, at the lowest level the group of village farmers will decide what is of prime importance to them to grow as a unit and for that they could identify breadth of their harvest basket (for easy marketing) as one criterion for assessing the top farmers or they could identify natural farming as another criteria (to improve the quality of their surrounding natural environment). On the other hand, the top farmers could benefit by winning employment opportunities for their family members or a higher share of the annual profits. As one may notice these are inspired from successful private models of operations where key performance indicators and a matching benefits package are the norm.

The objective is to identify the most progressive at each level and let them replicate their success at the next higher level. Apart from indicators of economic growth, commitment to social wealth, initiative etc. will be key to overall progress and all-round development of the farmer as well as the larger community.

Chapter - 06

THE PLATFORMS

A platform can mean many different things or ideas. Here we use it to denote the base on which all transactions between participating entities occur. It is the firm, robust structure that facilitates transactions. The platforms in our network can be online (completely internet based) or offline.

All transactions are for goods, services, information, money or labour. So, we will classify our platforms into one of these categories. To keep things simple, only those opportunities considered "low-hanging fruit" are mentioned here. These are the easiest to get started with and going.

Goods	• Retail company (grocery)
	• Inputs company (C&F retailers)
Information	• Multi-vendor online marketplace (like Amazon)
	• Online social network (like Facebook)
Services	• Logistics (goods movement)

Retail & Logistics

A retail company delivers physical goods to a consumer. The bulk of the transactions in growing economies is for groceries and vegetables. There are two reasons to establish this business. One is that there is a heavy volume of transactions from the farmers as consumers i.e. farmers are a huge consumer base for retail companies. So why not start our own retail business and eliminate the dependency on others? The second reason is that retailers are bulk purchasers of farm produce – cereals, millets, fruits, vegetables, etc. Why do farmers have to depend on others to sell their products when they themselves can do it and own a business? A typical farmer may shudder to think along these lines. But neither is it difficult nor is one farmer in this alone; neither is it costly nor will it eat the farmer's time; the farmer can be supported by professionals with expertise in these domains.

For the same reasons, running an input (chemicals, fertilizer, other farm inputs) company makes a lot of sense. Farmers are the largest customers for chemicals and fertilizers, seeds and other inputs to agriculture. The volume of transactions is huge and the potential of organizing actions around this business is a huge opportunity.

These high-volume businesses are heavily dependent on logistics services to protect the minimum margins. Along with retail, running a logistics business serves the purpose well; again, it can start small with no or minimal fixed assets. Running an in-house logistics business will immensely enable the group in the short-, mid- and long terms.

All these businesses need not start at the level of a million-dollar company; neither is it warranted nor necessary. It is enough to start small and then grow. It is prudent to follow this strategy because it is in the earliest stages of an enterprise that there will be a disproportionately high number of mistakes that may lead to losses.

Online marketplace

Farmers have been crippled by the poor quantity and quality of information that they can access or put out to the world. Information injustice is when someone who needs something cannot find it even when it is available somewhere with someone who cannot make its availability known. Farmers and consumers have endured this injustice for long. Today, it only takes an online multi-vendor marketplace for information to be made available globally. No one else is coming to fix this problem of the farmer; farmers must do this themselves. In today's environment, to get started with such a marketplace is unbelievably cheap.

Social network

While an online marketplace platform can be utilised for putting out structured data (details of products, etc.), there is still a lot of opportunity to share unstructured data, where the bulk of the knowledge and strategic advantage is. That is where an online social network finds its place. When innovative disruption could come from anyone from any direction and when multiple such disruptions are likely to see light in the larger eco-system, then facilitating interactions is the only way to realize the advantage. It is impossible to predict who will connect with who to bring out new ways of doing stuff. That is the reward of running a social network with the core objective of attaining a larger vision. Note that we are not only talking about farmers as the only entities to create connections here but also the village as a business entity and the customer as a word-of-mouth evangelist of a product, farmer or a village. Imagine a thousand village businesses (or more pompously, business villages) connecting to realize a larger vision. That is what this platform can achieve.

THE WHOLE, THE OUTPUT

SIGNIFICANCE, THE FOLK TALE

Once upon a time, there was a flock of doves that flew in search of food. As such the flock had flown a long distance and all the doves were hungry and tired. Finally, the doves sighted some rice grains scattered under a banyan tree.

All the doves were happy to find the food and happily landed on the ground. They started pecking, so happy to have a delicious food that they did not notice a net in the grass underneath their feet. Suddenly, the net closed around them, and they were trapped. The doves fluttered their wings, desperately trying to come out, but it was of no avail. Each dove used its fullest energy to get out of the net. But they tried individually, without organizing/ channelizing/ synchronizing their energies. They resigned to their fate that they will have to suffer because they did not have the energy to get out of the net. They blamed themselves for not having the energy to get out of the net.

Just then, they saw the hunter coming towards them. He appeared quite happy to find a huge number of doves trapped by the net. The whole flock was frightened and flapped their wings agitatedly on seeing the hunter. However, one of the old doves was very intelligent. He didn't lose his wisdom in the moment of ill-fate. He quickly devised a plan. He advised the doves, "In order to free ourselves from the net of this hunter, it is not enough to put our energy individually. We should all combine our energies and work for each other and work for the whole flock, if we have any chance of gaining our freedom. We must all flap together, use all our energy, and lift in unison. There is strength in unity. Now, come on; 3-2-1-go."

With their end nearing fast and hearing the old dove, all the doves flapped together with great synergy and were able to rise from the ground together like one huge bird, carrying the net with them. The hunter was shocked to see the birds flying along with the huge net. He ran after the birds, shouting madly, but could not catch them. Soon, they flew high over the hills and valleys, getting out of his sight and having realised the value of unity. Within a couple of minutes, their attitudes changed from blaming themselves for their fate to praising themselves for their united strength.

PARTICIPATE. STRUCTURE.

Just as the vertebral column provides the core structure to the human body, a structure is critical to any organization. The structure that is most suited for the vision of 'The farmer entrepreneur' is a network kind of a structure where each entity works as a separate independent unit but is firmly assisted and guided by an entity above.

	Village-level	District-level	State-level
Participating entity	Farmer	Village group	District group
No. of participants	10-50-100	5-10-50	5-10-30

The farmer participates in the activities and success of the village company. Typically, there will be 10 or 50 or 100 farmers participating in a village company.

Likewise, there will be 5 or 10 or up to 50 villages participating in the success of the district company. Similarly, there will be 5 or 10 or up to 30 districts contributing to the success of a state unit.

Village level

The first level is that of the farmer who has always been an entrepreneur in his own right. To realise the vision, the farmers within a village will come together to form a village company, a farmers producer company, a co-operative or, to start with, an informal group that can in time amalgamate into a company. This formal transition to an entrepreneur is key to realising the vision. It provides a set of advantages and specialised features that arm the farmer with the handle to (directly or indirectly) own, manage and run multiple businesses.

It is the farmer producer company that gives the legal right to a farmer to sell his products to anyone. Once that right is attained by all members of the village company, farmer groups across villages and districts can combine in various ways to share resources and organize effectively.

Farmers in the village

Core team & Responsibilities

From among the individual members, one or two farmers will volunteer to running the affairs of the company. There must be at least one full-time or part-time employee who will assist the village company to perform all tasks as planned. It is this employee that functions as the core engine of the company, especially in the initial days. In addition, there will be one representative from the district-level who will assist in the functioning of the village company by being an effective and efficient conduit between the district management and the village.

Village core team

Group leader

Full/ part-time employee (at least one)

District representative

At every level, there is a qualified resource that guides the entity in its performance. Every day, the farmer and the village will have doubts/ questions on how things work and need to be. The district representative in the core team will address all these issues and will be responsible for the overall performance of the village company. This is a critical role that the district representative will play.

Core Team Responsibilities

1. Set up the administrative necessities.

2. Build awareness among farmer members of the vision and the measures to make that a reality.

3. Set up weekly/ monthly goals for the core team and review the effectiveness. Showcase these to members.

4. Illustrate how vision is translated to action and how actions are bearing results and how results are bearing fruit.

5. Clear doubts about the structure, value and operations of the various units (district team, etc.).

6. Set up and fix targets for sales and purchases.

7. Plan budgets and maintain accounts.

8. Review and update the policies of the village team.

District level

Each village group formed in the preceding level will participate in the functioning of the district-level company/ federation/ group. Each village will have one representative in the district group. These representatives will actively participate in the framing of policies and structuring of operations of the district company. At least 60% of these representatives will be women farmers.

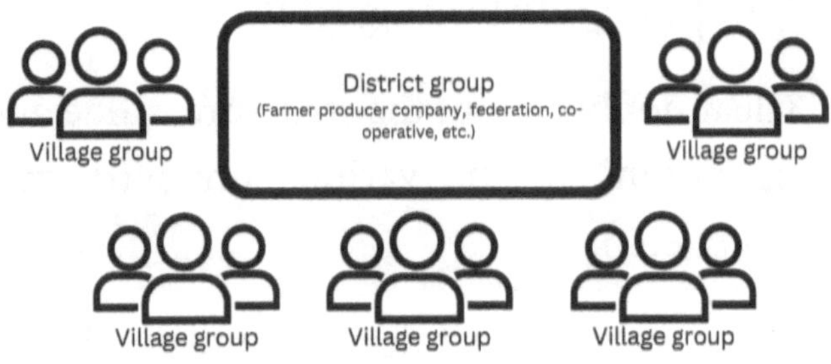

Core team

The district-level core team will be key to the effective functioning of the whole system. This team is in close contact with the village team and will have many opportunities to strengthen the core organisational capabilities. This team will know the pulse of the village teams. This team will be led by professional managers who will be responsible for the overall functioning of the district. They will have deep business knowledge and a keen understanding of agriculture systems in the district.

The core team will comprise of the representatives of the villages, the district management and full-time employees, representatives of group business companies and a state representative.

Similar to the role the district representative plays in the village company, the state representative will play a corresponding role in the district company. Every week, the district unit will have doubts/ questions on how things are and how they need to be. The state representative in the core team will address all these issues and will be responsible for the overall performance of the district company.

District core team

Core Team Responsibilities

Some of the core team's key responsibilities are:

1. Ensure a smooth functioning of the village groups in the district.

2. Handle sales and purchases at the district level.

3. Ensure village teams are trained to handle sales, purchases and accounts.

4. Ensure all group business companies are running smooth and their KPIs are met.

5. Ensure online platforms are utilised as envisioned. Remove bottlenecks to usage.

6. Liaise with state team to review and adjust targets.

Key Performance Indicators

Some of the KPIs of the district management team are:

1. Targets of village companies are met.

2. Sales and purchasing targets are met.

3. Group business companies are profitable.

4. Targets with respect to online platforms are met.

5. Monthly satisfaction ratings provided by village groups.

State level

Each district group formed in the preceding level within a state will participate in the functioning of the state-level company/ federation/ group. Each district will have one farmer representative in the state group. These representatives will actively participate in the framing of policies and structuring of operations of the state company. At least 60% of these representatives will be women farmers.

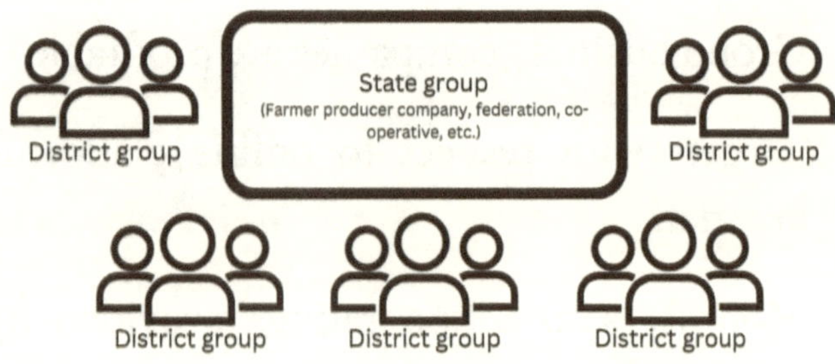

Core Team

The state-level core team will infuse discipline and ensure effectiveness across the whole "organisation" in the state. The progressiveness and creative juices of the collective farming community in that state will be reflected in the success of that state team. This team is in close contact with the apex decision-making body and will translate into action what was mere policy and direction. This team will be led by proven professional managers who will be responsible for the overall functioning of the state. The core team will comprise of the representatives of the districts, the state management and full-time employees, representatives of group business companies and a regional representative.

State core team

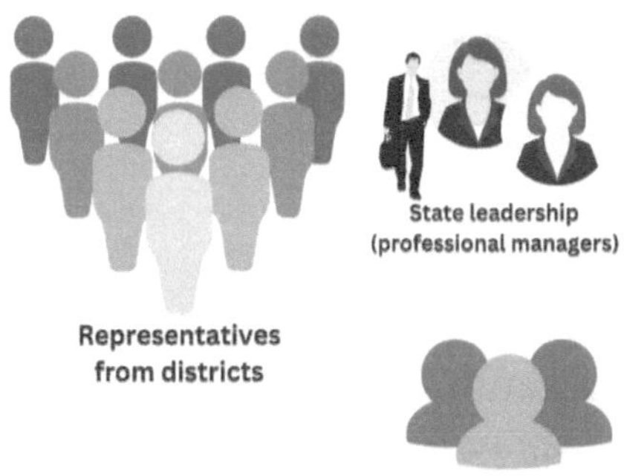

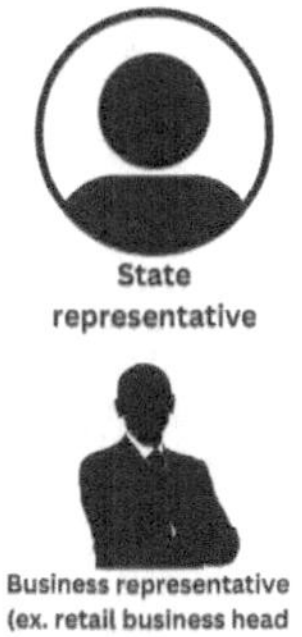

Core Team Responsibilities

Some of the responsibilities are:

1. Ensure all district teams are trained to fully deliver on planned activities.

2. Ensure targets of district teams are met and bottlenecks are resolved.

3. Develop policies compatible with state's requirements and needs.

4. Develop and pursue new business opportunities.

5. Conduct regular surveys on farmer member satisfaction.

6. Ensure business and social goals are met.

Regional level

The brain of the whole network of organizations is this top-level federation/ non-profit/ farmer company. This is the think-tank that devises strategies that are infallible and ensures the resources and power of the farmer are utilised optimally to benefit the farmer. This team will ensure that farmers are on the path towards realising the core vision. The primary members will be farmers who earn their living by agriculture. These members will actively participate in the framing of policies and structuring of operations of the regional group. At least 60% of these members will be women farmers. They will be ably supported by professionals and specialists across functions and sectors - chartered accountants, bankers, economists, technology professionals, social workers, media professionals, statisticians, etc. The brain power that is needed in today's business environment will be provided by this group.

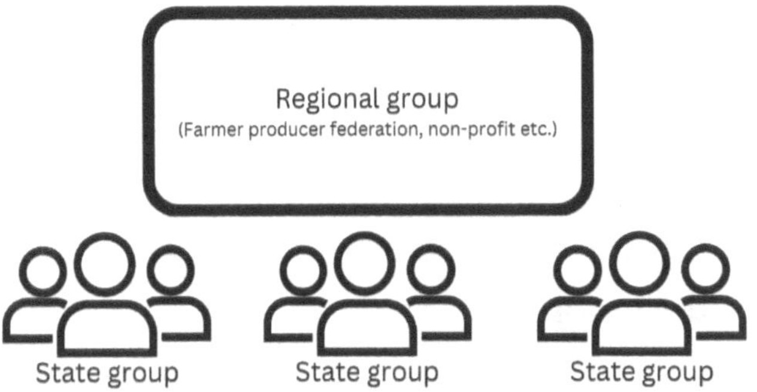

Core Team

The core team will be from among the most progressive farmers across states and specialists across disciplines, sectors and professions.

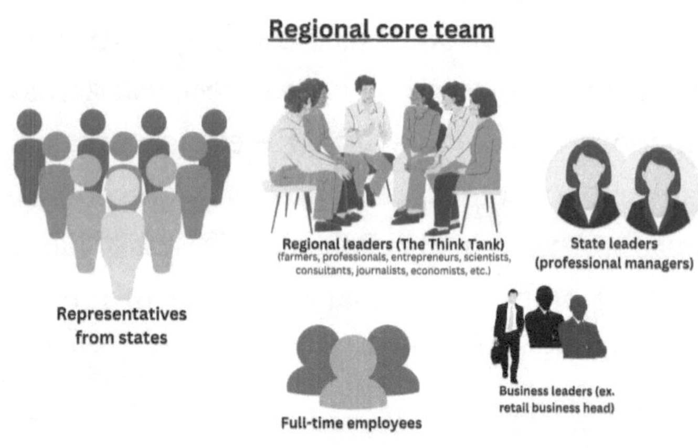

Core Team Responsibilities

Some of the key responsibilities are:

1. Ensure overall path and strategy to realising the vision.

2. Ensure online and offline platforms are functioning at peak levels.

3. Ensure the design of metrics to be followed at different levels is smooth.

4. Ensure business results are as planned.

5. Ensure the farmer member from the farthest corner is heard.

6. Ensure the flow of information across levels is smooth and immediate.

PERFORM. OPERATIONS.

Once the basic structure is in place, the primary objective of operations is that the district-level companies will be profitable from day-1. It is not so much about creating profits as much as it is about ascertaining that the foundation laid is right. Apart from the minimum level of business transactions that take place across the platforms, this will also ensure that expenses are planned and cost control across the eco-system is robust. Once districts give the desired results, the accounting of the village teams will be handled by the village teams themselves with training on key budgeting and accounting aspects.

Core engine

All operations will be in and around the core platforms mentioned earlier. The following flow diagram shows the minimum level of basic activities that will be needed to get the eco-system running. This is the core engine, the heartbeat, of the whole eco-system in many ways; as long and strong as this engine can run, the whole eco-system can flourish. For ease of understanding and space constraints, only one village is shown as using the online marketplace, but there are multiple villages across multiple districts across multiple states that will use the marketplace.

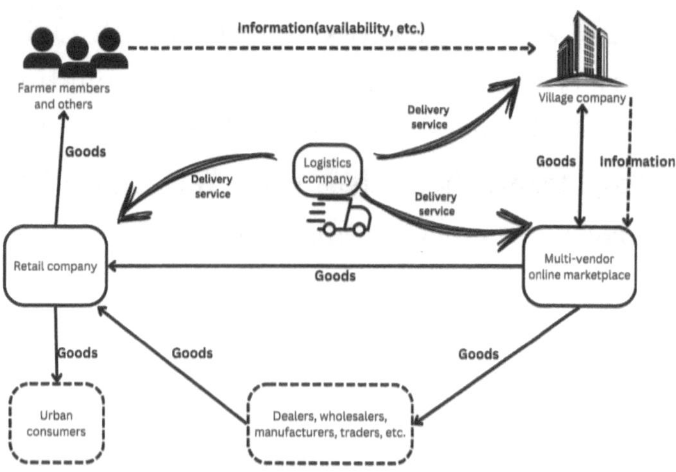

Role of farmers

The farmers purchase their regular essentials from the group's retail business. Also, they will ensure all their harvest-related information is updated in the marketplace against their village company. This is the mini version of the transactions that take place between farmers, the village company and the business companies.

Role of village company

The village company will ensure correct and accurate entry of all harvest information, prices, availability dates, etc. in the online marketplace. When they receive an order, the village company will use the policies they have framed to fulfil the order. There are many factors to be considered here but the main point is that the village company will fulfil the order as one unit just as any typical business does.

Role of marketplace

The online marketplace, run by the regional company, will provide accurate information to all parties concerned and complete all financial settlements after goods movement is completed based on the policies framed by the regional company/ top federation.

Role of retail company

The group's retail company will function as a stand-alone unit but, where and as much as possible, procure from the online marketplace. It will also procure from other manufacturers, dealers, etc. and fulfil orders from all consumers (farmer members and non-members, in villages, towns and cities).

Role of logistics company

All the above entities will need logistics services and the group's logistics company will fulfil these needs. It too will perform as a stand-alone unit entirely responsible for its own financial performance.

Central driver

The district company, the village company, the retail company, the farmers and all other participants will leverage the connections in the social network. Each will drive their core customer base into this social network. A multi-sided information exchange platform like this one will be the driver of sustainable growth in many ways going forward.

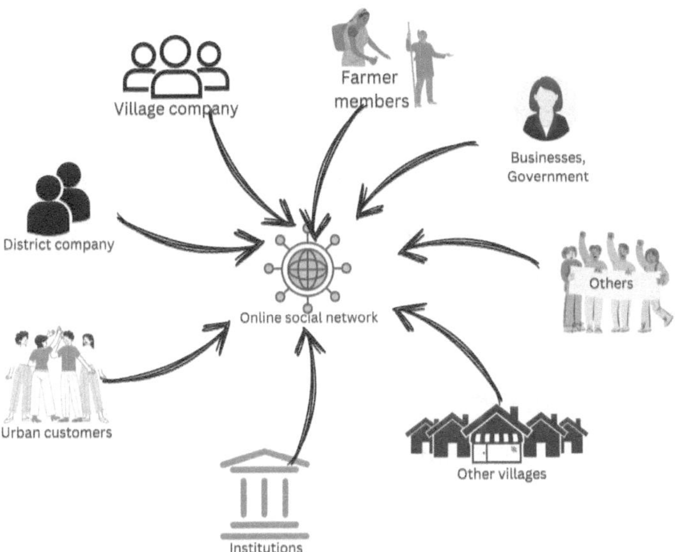

Some of the features and functions of this core network platform are as below:

1. This will be one key channel for improving awareness across the entire eco-system. Building awareness is not a one-time activity; it is an attitude that builds on itself. So, reinforcement of new methods, practices, processes over a long period is key and in time it will be a self-reinforcing mechanism.

2. Disseminate key happenings across the eco-system by being the go-to media.

3. Showcase top performers (farmers, villages, districts) to illustrate what is expected of each and what can be achieved.

4. Showcase and advertise each entity's uniqueness. Basically, create your identity and then establish your brand.

5. Connect with customers and business partners to drive sales on business platforms.

6. This will be a key channel for hiring the right talent.

7. This will be the key channel to launch special programmes (sports, awareness, brand-building, etc.)

PROGRESS. BENEFITS.

The one who participated and performed must progress. Stages 1 and 2 showed how one could participate and perform well. Finally, progress happens when factors of success are measured. What is not measured will probably never progress. So, what are the factors of success? The first and foremost factor is the amount of money (and debt) with the farmer and the village. Once there is a baseline of this, the performance of various entities (farmer, village company, district company, etc.) can be measured at different points of time to get an accurate sense of progress.

Then there are other contributing factors like the three pillars of action (awareness, unity, technology) that can be measured and that will have a direct correlation with progress.

The village-level company will be the primary locus of measurement of social progress. The performance of higher levels (district company, state company) will be measured by the aggregate performance of the lower-level entities plus the performance of the business entities at that level. Therefore, a district company will be a high performer if all the village companies under it are performing well, and differences are minimal. If there is a significant difference in performance of two village companies within a district, then probably the district company does not have much stake in the success of the high performing village company.

But performance evaluation and rewards criteria are not fixed anywhere and will always continue to mirror the larger environment and its evolution.

Evaluation system

<u>Factors of performance of individual members/ farmers:</u>

1. Purchases made from group companies (retail, etc.).

2. Sales made to village company.

3. Active participation in group platforms (social network, etc.).

4. Other factors determined by village company.

<u>Factors of performance of village company:</u>

1. Value of purchases made from individual farmer members.

2. Value of purchases/ sales made to/ fro other district and state companies.

3. Number of active farmer members.

4. Number of services provided to members.

5. Financial performance of the village company.

6. Number of special initiatives and their impact on members.

7. Active participation in affairs of the district company.

8. Number of employees provided to group companies.

9. Satisfaction score of farmer members and peer villages.

10. Other factors determined by district company.

<u>Factors of performance of district and state companies:</u>

How well all the village companies are performing will be the direct outcome of the performance of the district- and state-level companies. At the higher levels, apart from financial parameters, performance with respect to social impact will also be measured. For instance, how aware each farmer and her village is with respect to the overall vision will be key to overall progress in the long term.

Likewise, how well unity has been brought in among communities and how integrated the whole system is will be significant performance parameters. These factors will lead to a generally receptive attitude towards other community-driven social initiatives that will, in the long-term, lead to a healthy participative economic system.

Aside from the these, higher-level entities will also be measured by the performance of the group business companies (the core platforms) under their ambit. Ultimately, how each of these entities removes hurdles and enables their lower-level entities to stronger results will be the overall desired outcome. The hurdles that they need to work on will be different for district and state entities (ex. improving platform usage or training village groups on accounting or e-commerce platforms) but the outcomes are the effective and efficient utilisation of platforms.

Rewards system:

In today's companies, the key units in the rewards system are money (ex. annual bonus, salary hike, stock options), opportunities (ex. promotions, new challenges/ locations) and power (ex. promotion, leadership roles). So will it be in our network. Once each entity is weighed based on its performance, it will have a relative score in each evaluation cycle. Based on that score, each entity can claim it's reward. Broadly, the rewards are:

1. Profits: a share of the profits of the group business companies (ex. retail).

2. Stocks: a share of the stocks of group companies and new companies.

3. Employment: preferential treatment for their family members/ village/ district in vacancies of group companies.

4. Stronger say and/ or leadership in the next higher-level company.

5. Contribution fee: to individual contributors for their significant performance.

There are various ways of structuring the rewards package and it can be reviewed from time to time. But this is a starting point to give an idea of how rewards can look like.

Part-III:

THE MOVEMENT

PRINCIPLES AND PILLARS IN ACTION

When you identify a need for a product or service, acquire the product (by manufacturing or purchasing wholesale) and sell it to those who want it, that is a business. When this is done in an economically sustainable way (cost of running the business is less than the margin), then you may have a profitable, successful, competitive and sustainable business.

Suppose there is a demand for bread in your village and there are at least 100 loaves (units) sold by a hawker every week.

Demand/ week = 100 units

Suppose you find a wholesaler who can deliver 100 units at Rs. 30 to you; you want to sell each for Rs. 40.

Purchase cost = 30 x 100 = Rs. 3,000

In order to beat the competition, you offer a discount of Rs. 2 on the sales price of Rs. 40. You are able to sell all the units that week.

Total sales/ week = 38 x 100 = Rs. 3,800

Total sales/ month = 3,800 x 4 = Rs. 15,200

The difference between the revenue (sales) and the purchase cost is the margin.

Margin/ week = 3,800 – 3,000 = Rs. 800

Margin/ month = 800 x 4 = Rs. 3,200

All the expenses of running the business must be met using this amount and there, preferably, must be a surplus.

You have engaged a person on part-time basis to vend/ deliver and maintain the accounts. That employee is paid Rs. 200/ week.

Wages/ week = Rs. 200

Wages/ month = 200 x 4 = Rs. 800

You have rented a small shop at a monthly rent of Rs. 500.

Rent = Rs. 500 / month

After one month, all the incomes and expenses are listed as below. This is called the income statement.

Sales	15,200	Revenue
Purchases	12,000	Acquisition cost
Margin	3,200	Revenue - Purchases
Wages	800	Expense 1
Rent	500	Expense 2
Profit	1,900	Margin - Expenses

This is the rhythm of every business, big and small.

The complexity of managing a business arises due to the inevitable increase in the numbers of every entity above – product, supplier, employees, goods purchases/ receipts, goods sales/ issues, expenses, amount payments to vendors, amount receipts from customers, etc.; acquiring a product could happen with wholesale purchase or manufacturing, where the complexity is even more.

One may be excited and want to start a business right away. But if everyone wants to run it, then no one will be buying from the other resulting in a loss to everyone. It is enough to let the village company run this business and support it by being a loyal customer.

COALESCE

Five villages in your district are able to procure bread from a supplier and sell it in their villages. These villages understand how business works as they have run this business profitably for many months now.

These five villages have come together to operate the same business at the district level. For this purpose, they have formed a district level business entity that will oversee and be responsible for all operations and profitability of the new business. The business entity finds that there is a demand for 4,000 units of bread per week in the main town of 10,000 households. The entity estimates that they can meet the demand of 500 units out of 4,000 units with a cost increase of 50%. To do this, the group rents a storage area and employs their current resources (from the villages) and hires other resources as needed.

So, the new entity will sell 500 units apart from the 500 units in the villages. The total quantity sold is 1,000 units per week in the district.

Quantity sold in 4 weeks = 1,000 x 4 weeks

Total quantity sold = 4,000 units

Revenue = 4,000 x 38 = Rs. 1,52,000

Purchases = 4,000 x 30 = Rs. 1,20,000

Margin = 32,000

Expenses = 1,300 x 5 villages = Rs. 6,500

Costs in town (50% higher) = 50% of 6,500 = Rs. 3,250

Total expenses = Rs. 9,750

Profit = 32,000 – 9,750 = 22,250

Profit for each village = 22,250 / 5 = Rs. 4,450

Sales	1,52,000	*Revenue*
Purchases	1,20,000	*Acquisition cost*
Margin	32,000	*Revenue – Purchases*
Wages	4000	*Expense 1*
Rent	2500	*Expense 2*
Town	3,250	*Town expenses*
Profit	22,250	*Margin – Expenses*
Profit/ village	4,450	*Profit/ No. of villages*

The profit that was Rs. 1,900 for each village has increased to Rs. 4,450 by expanding to the nearest town. Can the profits increase even more by operating at the state level?

State level

Five districts in state are able to procure bread from suppliers and sell it in their districts. These district entities have run the bread retailing business profitably for many months now.

These five districts have come together to operate the same business at the state level. For this purpose, they have formed a state-level business entity that will oversee and be responsible for all operations and profitability of the new state-level business.

The current sales quantity is 20,000 units per month across the five districts. The new state entity estimates that sales can at least be doubled by focusing on new towns and cities across the state. The entity also recommends manufacturing bread in the food park established by the state government. It estimates that the cost of production will be Rs. 15 per unit with a capacity of 1,00,000 units per month. The state entity estimates that they can double the sales on a cost increase of 80%. In effect, there will be a profitable (from day 1) and independent bread manufacturing business run by professionals in the baking/ food industry; there is also the bread retailing business that will operate profitably (from day 1) at the state level.

Ultimately, the businesses will result in the profits to the villages increasing manifold.

CLOSE THE LOOP

The state group finds that the bulk of the input costs are for procuring wheat, which is the main ingredient in bread. They source all the wheat from the multivendor online marketplace, which is one of the core platforms in this ecosystem. The farmers in our districts upload all the upcoming harvest information into the online marketplace and the bread manufacturing business is mandated by the farmers to source 100% of the input needs from the marketplace.

The bread manufacturing company and the bread retailing company are completely owned by the 25 villages (in our five districts). So, the profits of the bread companies belong to the owners of the companies i.e. the 25 villages.

Income statement of bread manufacturing company

Production = 40,000 units / month

Cost of production = 15 x 40,000 = Rs. 6,00,000

Other expenses like logistics/ distribution, etc. = Rs. 8/ unit

Total of other expenses = 8 x 40,000 = Rs. 3,20,000

Revenue from sales = 30 x 40,000 = Rs. 12,00,000

Sales	12,00,000	Revenue
Production	6,00,000	Acquisition cost
Margin	6,00,000	Revenue – Production
Logistics, etc.	3,20,000	Expenses
Profit	2,80,000	Margin – Expenses

Income statement of bread retailing company

Total quantity sold = 40,000 units

Revenue = 40,000 x 38 = Rs. 15,20,000

Purchases = 40,000 x 30 = Rs. 12,00,000

Margin = 3,20,000

Expenses = 1,300 x 25 villages = Rs. 32,500

Costs in towns (80% higher) = 80% of 32,500 = Rs. 26,000

Total expenses = Rs. 58,500

Profit = 3,20,000 – 58,500 = 2,61,500

Sales	15,20,000	Revenue
Purchases	12,00,000	Acquisition cost
Margin	3,20,000	Revenue – Purchases
Expenses	58,500	Expenses
Profit	2,61,500	Margin – Expenses

Overall profit from both companies

Manufacturing profit	2,80,000
Retailing profit	2,61,500
Total profit	5,41,500
Total profit/ village	541500/ 25 = 21,660

Thus, the profit to each village will increase from Rs. 1,900 (operating at village level) to Rs. 4,450 (operating at district level) to Rs. 21,660 (operating at the state level) by expanding operations by combining with other farmers across geographies.

It must be noted here that the loop has been closed – the farmers have sold their wheat to the bread company in such a way that the terms of the sale always favour the farmers. Also, preference is given in employment to the family members of the farmers in the village companies.

ORGANIZATIONAL PRODUCTION

By now, the farmers in our villages will have a nuanced understanding, an acute awareness, of the significance of demand in the production process. By knowing how much of wheat will be needed by the bread manufacturing company next year, farmers and the village company will know how much to produce.

Production and consumption are two sides of the same coin. There cannot be consumption without production and without consumption, production is either non-existent or wasteful.

Till now, the village company has been a vehicle where farmers have come together and exercised the power of their consumption i.e. they have channelised and organized their consumption. With that as the lever, they have utilised the power of business to expand their reach and increase their earnings.

Farmers have not utilised the power of the other side of the coin – production i.e. they have still not channelised and organized their production activities.

In a typical manufacturing company, like a bread manufacturer or a car manufacturer, all production activities begin with the order/demand estimates and operational control. Operational control simply means ensuring

➢ timely availability of the right inputs and

➢ timely execution of the right processes

A village company can either assist the individual farmers in their production activities or take their farms on rent and centralise all production activities. When a village company takes ownership of production activities, bringing in operational control becomes much easier and effective.

By centralizing production activities, individual farmers save themselves from the daily stresses, strains and financial costs of managing all aspects of production, post-harvest and sales processes. In return, they can also gain employment income, rental income and a share of the production profits in proportion to land, labour and capital contributed.

IMAGINE. IGNITE.

Farmers have become deeply aware, strongly united and technology enabled. They know how corporations are run, and they have been running many profitable businesses for years now. They innately believe that only they can solve their problems and if need be, they can solve others' problems too. They have a strong handle to protect and grow their economic and social well-being in any kind of a changing socio-economic scenario. They live freely without any dependence on anyone for anything.

The first and most important social infrastructure they strengthened is the education of their children. They ensured the best and most passionate teachers were hired to teach in their schools.

The village company takes off all the burden of managing farm activities and all other quotidian tasks. The village company ensures that the farmer's life is eminently bearable and flourishing, financial security being the last of her worries.

Villages become immaculate hotspots of innovation and opportunity, tradition and culture, education, progressive modernity and peace to where everyone wants to belong.

Starting with the village company, farmers have coalesced and collaborated at different and higher levels and are now in control of many corporate businesses. The whole economy is in the clutches of the farmer entrepreneur. Consequently, she is able to not only influence, but also determine, public policy.

The farmer has everything in her power. Nonetheless, by virtue of being close to nature and in correspondence with it on a daily basis, she lives a simple, down-to-earth life, content with what she has, and kind and sensitive enough to help those in need. She, now, turns her attention to the most pressing issues of society. She is able to imagine solutions to those and is able to rally support, gather resources, and bring together any party to implement solutions with her sheer power and Gandhian ethos. She resolves long-running conflicts and long-pending disputes.

She heralds the era of perpetual justice and peace.

A PRAYER

Over the past decade, I have poured my heart and soul into this work and of what remained I have poured it now into this book. I rest my case with the farmer - the old and the new, the rich and the poor, the big and the small, the one located far and near, the educated and the illiterate… Your strength is in the community, the community's in you. Open your eyes to the hardships and helplessness, not of yours but to another's across the country. Only on your arrival, the world can thrive, in justice and peace.

AUTHOR BIO

Santhosh Lakshmanan comes from a tiny agricultural village in Nilgiri district of Tamilnadu in India. An Engineer who worked in the software industry for about 10 years, he had always been aware of the problems of farmers.

In 2014, at the age of 33, he started to work on his theory of change. Two years into agriculture and entrepreneurship, he not only was convinced that solutions to farm distress can only be solved by farmers themselves, but he also came to firmly believe that farmers were the only section of people who could, by taking control of their businesses, determine a just and new world order through their progressive actions.

It struck him that the farmer can combine entrepreneurship in hitherto unimagined ways on a broad scale. It is these ways he created models for and tested within his home district. He tested the end-to-end agriculture and business chain processes; he reared cattle, took up farm production, marketed and sold farm produce to retail and business customers and delivered goods across 40 villages; he set up retail and food businesses, and operated a rudimentary multi-vendor online marketplace platform and an online social network.

All these proved to him that these, and many other, businesses can be owned and leveraged by farmers to empower themselves. It is the underlying principles, pillars of action and the generic method behind these activities that he has condensed into his book 'The Farmer Entrepreneur'.

* 9 7 9 8 8 9 5 1 9 8 6 4 3 *